D1165083

U.S. NAVY

FIGHTING FORCES

JASON COOPER

Vero Beach, Florida 32964

© 2004 Rourke Publishing LLC

www.rourkepublishing.com

PHOTO CREDITS: Title page, pp. 4, 5, 13, 22 courtesy U.S. Navy; pp. 7, 14, 17 courtesy Defense Visual Information Center; pp. 9, 18, 21, 25, 26, 28 courtesy National Archives; p.11 courtesy U.S. Naval Academy

Title page: *A Navy SEAL signals an OK to his crewmembers.*

Editor: Frank Sloan

Cover and page design by Nicola Stratford

Library of Congress Cataloging-in-Publication Data

Cooper, Jason, 1942-
  U.S. Navy / Jason Cooper.
      v. cm. — (Fighting forces)
Includes bibliographical references and index.
Contents: What the U.S. Navy does — The U.S. Navy at work — The Navy Command — Life in the Navy — Naval ships — Naval planes — The Navy's beginnings.
  ISBN 1-58952-716-X (hardcover)
  1. United States. Navy—Juvenile literature. [1. United States. Navy.] I. Title. II. Series: Cooper, Jason, 1942-   Fighting forces.
  VA58.4.C66 2003
  359'.00973—dc21
                                                  2003005283

Printed in the USA

CG/CG

TABLE OF CONTENTS

WHAT THE U.S. NAVY DOES

CHAPTER ONE

Each of America's **armed services** helps defend the country in a special way. The U.S. Navy is the nation's armed force of the seas. The Navy's job is to defend America and her interests on, above, and below the seas.

▲ *Sailors wheel a cart carrying laser-guided bombs for an F/A-18 Hornet aboard the aircraft carrier* USS *Enterprise.*

The Navy does its job with the world's most powerful **fleet** of warships. Among the Navy's warships are giant aircraft carriers longer than three football fields!

The Navy, of course, is more than ships and planes, rockets, torpedoes, missiles, and bombs. The Navy is people—nearly 400,000 men and women serving on active duty. The Navy has about 160,000 more men and women in the naval **reserve**. The Navy has another 185,000 **civilian** workers. Civilians are not members of the armed services.

Navy specialists ▶ *track ships from their computer stations aboard the USS John Kennedy.*

CHAPTER TWO

THE U.S. NAVY AT WORK

During wartime, the Navy's main job is to find and destroy the enemy. The "enemy" could be another surface ship or submarine. It could be an airplane, big guns, or enemy soldiers.

The Navy is clearly built to fight if it must. But one reason for having a powerful U.S. Navy is to prevent war. Most nations do not want to challenge the American Navy.

Even in peacetime the Navy has several important jobs. Naval ships can make a show of force to change another nation's behavior. Just the arrival of an American aircraft carrier can help cool off a dangerous situation. The peacetime Navy brings food and emergency supplies to victims of **disasters**. It also helps ships that are in trouble.

▲ *Navy ships can be sent around the world. Here the Abraham Lincoln sails toward Valparaiso, Chile.*

CHAPTER THREE

THE NAVY COMMAND

The Department of the Navy operates the Navy. The same department operates the U.S. Marine Corps. The Department of the Navy is part of the American government's Department of Defense. The Department of Defense manages the U.S. Navy, Air Force, Army, and Marines.

The Navy boss is the secretary of the Navy. The secretary of the Navy is a civilian. The secretary of the Navy answers to the secretary of the Department of Defense.

The secretary of Defense answers to the president of the United States. The president is commander-in-chief of all the American armed forces.

HIGHEST RANKS
IN DESCENDING ORDER
ADMIRAL
VICE ADMIRAL
REAR ADMIRAL
CAPTAIN
COMMANDER
LIEUTENANT COMMANDER
LIEUTENANT
LIEUTENANT JUNIOR GRADE
ENSIGN

▲ *President Franklin D. Roosevelt (white shirt), General Douglas MacArthur, Admiral Chester Nimitz, and Admiral W.D. Leahy meet to make war plans in 1944.*

CHAPTER FOUR

Men and women join the Navy for many reasons. Some simply want to serve the nation by being in one of the armed forces. Others seek adventure, travel, or job training. Many navy people live aboard ships that travel to faraway places. But not everyone who joins the Navy will see the world by sea. The Navy has land bases and many jobs that will not make anyone seasick.

People can join the Navy from ages 17 to 34. They must pass the Navy's physical and written tests. People who join the Navy do so for a term of four to six years.

Naval life begins with several weeks of training at a naval "boot camp." Recruits learn Navy discipline and basic skills, such as **seamanship**.

FACT FILE

A FEW EXCEPTIONAL SAILORS MAKE UP THE NAVY SEALS (SEA, AIR, AND LAND). THE SEALS TAKE PART IN VERY DANGEROUS AND SECRET NAVY MISSIONS. THE SEALS ARE ONE OF THE UNITS IN AMERICA'S SPECIAL OPERATIONS FORCES.

Many naval officers begin their careers at the U.S. Naval Academy in Annapolis, Maryland. Another path to becoming a naval officer is the Reserve Officer Training Corps (ROTC). The ROTC program allows students to attend a college of their choice and become officers.

▲ *The Color Guard of the U.S. Naval Academy carries flags past academy students called midshipmen.*

CHAPTER FIVE

NAVAL SHIPS

The U.S. Navy's strength lies in its well-trained sailors, modern planes, and ships. The Navy has more than 300 ships. They include aircraft carriers, guided missile cruisers, destroyers, submarines, and helicopter and troop carriers. The Navy also has several kinds of **amphibious** ships. Amphibious ships move equipment and **Marines** from sea to shore. They also transport helicopters.

The largest of the Navy's warships are aircraft carriers. Their long, flat decks have earned them the nickname "flattops." Carrier decks are floating runways. Once aboard, airplanes are removed to a lower deck by elevator. Carrier plane wings fold up to save space.

The Navy has 12 aircraft carriers. The largest U.S. carriers are the largest warships in the world. They carry 85 airplanes and have **crews** of more than 5,500 sailors.

▲ *An F/A-18C Hornet readies for takeoff aboard the aircraft carrier USS* George Washington.

One of the most famous kinds of warship is the battleship. Japan's surrender to the United States at the end of World War II (1939-1945) was made aboard the battleship *Missouri.* Another famous American battleship was the *Arizona*. It was sunk by Japanese planes on December 7, 1941, in Pearl Harbor, Hawaii. It remains where it sank. Thousands of people visit the *Arizona* Memorial each year.

◀ *The USS* Pennsylvania *and another battleship, followed by three cruisers, enter the Lingayen Gulf, Philippine Islands, in January, 1945.*

CHAPTER SIX

NAVAL PLANES

World War II showed that air power at sea could sometimes cripple the mightiest surface ships. Therefore the U.S. Navy has built much of its strength around submarines, aircraft carriers, and more than 4,000 aircraft. Navy airplanes fly both from coastal land bases and naval ships.

The swiftest naval jets are F-14 Tomcat fighter-bombers and FA-18 Hornet fighters. Tomcats can fly at more than twice the speed of sound. That's more than 1,300 miles (2,080 kilometers) per hour.

Navy bombers from a carrier drop bombs on Hokadate, Japan, in July, 1945, shortly before the end of World War II. ▶

▲ *An F-14 Tomcat blasts off the deck of the aircraft carrier USS* Independence.

The Navy's fighters and fighter-bombers are designed to attack enemy planes, ships, and ground targets.

The Navy's EA-6B Prowler aircraft helps protect Navy attack planes. It has high-tech electronic equipment to jam enemy **radar** and conversations.

The E-2C Hawkeye can fly in any type of weather. Its electronic gear gives Navy planes and ships early warning of enemy activity. It collects information to help Navy officers make decisions.

The SH-60 Seahawk is a helicopter used by both the Navy and Marine Corps. The Seahawk can be used for rescue work and to attack submarines and ships.

During Operation Iraqi Freedom in the spring of 2003, hundreds of Navy jets flying from aircraft carriers made daily raids against targets in Iraq.

CHAPTER SEVEN

THE NAVY'S BEGINNINGS

In 1775 the Continental Congress created the Continental Navy. Congress took several wooden ships used by traders. It mounted guns on them and called them warships.

By the end of the war against England, America had about 60 ships in her little navy. America won the Revolutionary War (1775-1783) largely on land. Keeping a navy, somehow, did not seem important. By 1785, the new United States was out of the naval business altogether.

FACT FILE ★

THE NAVY CAME BACK TO LIFE IN 1794. THE GOVERNMENT VOTED TO BUILD SEVERAL WOODEN WARSHIPS TO PROTECT AMERICAN TRADING SHIPS. IN 1798 CONGRESS CREATED THE NAVY DEPARTMENT. BY 1801 THE NAVY HAD ABOUT 50 SHIPS.

The USS Constitution *captures the British* Guerriere *during the War of 1812.*

But interest in keeping a powerful navy did not last. A second war with England, the War of 1812 (1812-1815), began. The United States had just 16 warships when the war started. Several naval battles were fought during the War of 1812. The American warship *Constitution* survived the war and is still kept in sailing condition by the Navy. You can visit the *Constitution* in Boston, Massachusetts.

▲ *The first American ironclad gunboat was the* Saint Louis, *built in 1862, during the Civil War.*

Later, during the Civil War (1861-1865), the U.S. Navy played a huge role. The Northern states used the Navy to block other ships from entering coastal cities in the South. By the war's end, the Union (Northern) Navy was the world's largest and most powerful fleet.

America entered World War I (1914-1918) in the spring of 1917. The U.S. Navy ships carried more than two million American soldiers to Europe. Amazingly, not a single American soldier died from enemy fire on those trips. Shortly after the war, the United States sailed her first aircraft carrier.

On December 7, 1941, U.S. Navy warships at Pearl Harbor took tremendous losses from Japanese bombers. That attack brought the United States into World War II (1939-1945). In June, 1942, airplanes from American aircraft carriers destroyed several Japanese warships near Midway Island.

▲ *The USS* Shaw *explodes during the Japanese attack on Pearl Harbor, December 7, 1941.*

The Japanese Navy never recovered. America had begun to take command of the Pacific Ocean. Carrier planes raided Japanese targets. American subs attacked enemy shipping. Battleships bombarded targets on islands held by the Japanese. Meanwhile, the U.S. Navy grew increasingly larger and more powerful.

The U.S. Navy has far fewer ships and sailors today. But what it lacks in numbers, it makes up for with punch. Today's modern U.S. Navy is the most powerful in the world.

GLOSSARY

amphibious (am FIB ee us) — of use both on land and sea

armed services (AHRMED SUR vuh sez) — the military forces of a government, such as the U.S. Navy

civilian (suh VIL yun) — one who is not a member of the armed forces

crews (CREWZ) — the people who together operate a particular plane or ship

disasters (duh ZASS turz) — events of great destruction

fleet (FLEET) — a large group of ships, especially warships

Marines (muh REENZ) — members of the U.S. Marine Corps, a military service in partnership with the Navy

radar (RAY dahr) — a system of radio beams through which objects in flight can be discovered before they are seen

reserve (ree SURV) — non-active soldiers who may be called to active duty in a national emergency

seamanship (SEE mun SHIP) — knowledge of the sea and sailing

INDEX

FURTHER READING

Abramovitz, Melissa. *The U.S. Navy at War.* Capstone, 2001

Gaines, Ann Graham. *The Navy in Action.* Enslow, 2001

Payan, Gregory, and Alexander Guelke. *Life on a Submarine.* Children's Press, 2000

WEBSITE TO VISIT

www.navy.mil

ABOUT THE AUTHOR

Jason Cooper has written several children's books about a variety of topics for Rourke Publishing, including the recent series *Eye to Eye with Big Cats* and *Holiday Celebrations*.